AF420518

The Energy Equation

The Energy Equation

Matthew Petchinsky

The Energy Equation: Maximize Your Output Without Burning Out

By: Matthew Petchinsky

Introduction: The Power of Energy Over Time

In our modern world, time has become the ultimate currency. People rush through their days, fixating on the ticking clock and trying to cram as much as possible into every hour. Yet, despite the obsession with managing time, burnout, fatigue, and inefficiency plague many of us. Why? Because we've overlooked a crucial truth: **energy, not time, is the true foundation of productivity, creativity, and well-being.**

Why Energy Matters More Than Time

Time is a finite resource—24 hours in a day, no more, no less. Energy, however, is dynamic and replenishable. The difference lies in how you feel during the time you have. One hour of focused, energized effort can accomplish more than an entire day of sluggish, distracted work. Without energy, even the most meticulously planned schedule becomes meaningless.

When you operate with high energy, everything flows seamlessly. Decisions are sharper, creativity soars, and challenges feel surmountable. On the other hand, low energy makes even small tasks seem monumental. This is why energy management is not just a productivity hack—it's a fundamental life skill. By prioritizing energy, you reclaim control over how you experience time.

Energy also transcends mere physical stamina. It encompasses mental clarity, emotional resilience, and spiritual alignment. When these aspects are in harmony, you tap into a deeper reserve of vitality—one that fuels not just your actions but your passion, purpose, and fulfillment.

How to Tap Into Your Limitless Energy Reserves

The idea of limitless energy might sound far-fetched, but it's entirely achievable when you understand its sources and learn how to cultivate them. Unlike time, which you cannot create or extend, energy can be renewed, amplified, and channeled intentionally. Here are the foundational principles to unlock your infinite energy potential:

1. **Optimize Your Physical Energy**

   Your body is your energy powerhouse, and its care is non-negotiable. Nutrition, hydration, sleep, and exercise form the core pillars of physical vitality. Eating energy-rich, nutrient-dense foods, staying hydrated, maintaining consistent sleep cycles, and engaging in regular movement all help recharge your energy reserves. Treat your body like the high-performance machine it is, and it will reward you with sustained stamina and strength.

2. **Master Your Mental Energy**

   Cluttered thoughts and constant distractions deplete your energy faster than any physical activity. By decluttering your mind, focusing on priorities, and practicing mindfulness, you conserve and direct your mental energy toward meaningful tasks. Techniques like journaling, meditation, and deep work help sharpen focus and prevent mental fatigue.

3. **Cultivate Emotional Energy**

   Emotional energy is often overlooked, yet it plays a critical role in how you feel and perform. Negative emotions like anger, anxiety, and resentment drain your energy, while positive emotions like gratitude, joy, and love rejuvenate it. Building emotional resilience through practices like gratitude journaling, emotional regulation, and fostering meaningful relationships keeps your energy vibrant.

4. **Align with Your Purpose**

Spiritual energy arises when you connect deeply with your purpose and values. When your actions align with your core beliefs and aspirations, energy flows effortlessly. This alignment eliminates the fatigue that stems from resistance and indecision, replacing it with a sense of fulfillment and drive.

5. **Embrace Micro-Replenishment**

Small, intentional pauses throughout your day—like taking a few deep breaths, stepping outside for fresh air, or practicing a 5-minute meditation—can work wonders for replenishing your energy. These micro-moments of rest prevent burnout and keep your reserves steady.

6. **Eliminate Energy Vampires**

Some habits, relationships, and environments drain energy without adding value. Identifying and eliminating these "energy vampires" creates space for activities and people that uplift and energize you. This could mean setting boundaries, reducing screen time, or surrounding yourself with positive influences.

By mastering these principles, you'll discover that energy isn't a finite resource but a renewable one that's within your control. This book will serve as your guide to unlocking and sustaining this energy, empowering you to break free from the constraints of time and live a life that feels limitless.

In the chapters ahead, we'll dive deep into actionable strategies, transformative practices, and mindset shifts that will help you harness your energy reserves. By the end of this journey, you'll not only understand why energy matters more than time—you'll embody it, living a life that's more productive, fulfilling, and vibrant than you ever imagined.

Let's begin.

Chapter 1: The Energy Audit

Before you can master your energy, you need to understand where it's going. Just like a financial audit helps you identify spending patterns, an energy audit reveals how you're using and losing your energy throughout the day. By identifying energy drains and pinpointing energy boosters, you'll uncover hidden patterns and gain actionable insights to reclaim control over your vitality.

Identifying Your Energy Drains

Energy drains are the activities, habits, environments, or even people that leave you feeling depleted. While some drains are obvious—like staying up too late or overworking—others are more subtle and insidious, gradually eroding your energy without you even realizing it. Here's how to systematically identify what's sapping your energy:

1. **Track Your Daily Energy Levels**
   Start by keeping a journal or using an energy-tracking app to log how you feel at different times of the day. Note when your energy dips and what you were doing beforehand. Pay attention to patterns: Are you always tired after certain meetings, activities, or interactions?

2. **Examine Your Physical Habits**
   - **Sleep:** Are you getting enough restorative sleep? Poor sleep quality is one of the biggest energy drains.
   - **Nutrition:** Do you rely on sugary snacks or caffeine for quick energy boosts? These can lead to crashes later.
   - **Exercise:** Too little or too much exercise can sap your vitality. Find a balance that energizes rather than exhausts you.

3. **Analyze Your Mental Habits**
   - **Overthinking:** Constant worrying or overanalyzing drains mental energy.
   - **Multitasking:** Switching between tasks reduces efficiency and increases fatigue.

- **Negative Self-Talk:** Internal criticism consumes energy that could be directed toward constructive actions.

4. **Identify Emotional Triggers**
   - **Toxic Relationships:** Interactions with draining people—those who are overly critical, demanding, or negative—can leave you emotionally exhausted.
   - **Unresolved Conflicts:** Lingering arguments or unspoken frustrations weigh on your emotional reserves.
   - **Stress:** High levels of unmanaged stress drain both your mental and physical energy.

5. **Evaluate Environmental Factors**
   - **Clutter:** A disorganized workspace or home can contribute to mental fatigue.
   - **Noise:** Constant background noise, whether from electronics or your surroundings, can be mentally draining.
   - **Lighting:** Poor lighting, especially artificial blue light from screens, can disrupt your circadian rhythm and deplete energy over time.

Pinpointing Energy Boosters

Just as some activities and habits drain your energy, others recharge and amplify it. Energy boosters are unique to each individual, so it's essential to discover what works best for you. Here's how to uncover and enhance your sources of vitality:

1. **Recognize What Energizes You**

   Reflect on moments when you've felt vibrant, focused, and alive. What were you doing? Who were you with? How did your environment contribute? Examples might include:
   - Engaging in a creative hobby.
   - Spending time with loved ones.
   - Immersing yourself in nature.

2. **Enhance Physical Energy Boosters**
   - **Hydration:** Drinking enough water throughout the day is a simple but powerful energy booster.
   - **Balanced Nutrition:** Foods rich in whole grains, lean protein, and healthy fats provide sustained energy.
   - **Movement:** Short bursts of activity, such as a quick walk or stretching, can invigorate both body and mind.

3. **Cultivate Mental Energy Boosters**
   - **Mindfulness Practices:** Techniques like meditation, deep breathing, or yoga can restore focus and calm.
   - **Learning New Skills:** Challenging your mind with new knowledge or skills keeps your brain engaged and energized.
   - **Clear Priorities:** Setting daily intentions and focusing on high-impact tasks reduces mental clutter.

4. **Nurture Emotional Energy Boosters**
   - **Gratitude Practice:** Regularly reflecting on things you're grateful for can shift your emotional state and recharge your energy.
   - **Acts of Kindness:** Helping others often boosts your own emotional well-being.
   - **Positive Relationships:** Surrounding yourself with supportive, uplifting people creates a cycle of mutual energy enhancement.

5. **Leverage Environmental Energy Boosters**
   - **Declutter Your Space:** A clean, organized environment can reduce mental distractions and improve focus.
   - **Fresh Air and Natural Light:** Spending time outdoors or opening a window to let in sunlight can immediately uplift your mood and energy.
   - **Soothing Sounds or Scents:** Listening to calming music or using aromatherapy (e.g., lavender or citrus scents) can create an energizing atmosphere.

How to Conduct Your Energy Audit

Performing an energy audit involves assessing your daily activities, habits, and environments to identify both drains and boosters. Here's a step-by-step guide:

1. **Log Your Activities**

   Over the course of a week, record everything you do, from waking up to going to bed. Include both major activities (e.g., work tasks, social events) and minor ones (e.g., scrolling through your phone, commuting).

2. **Rate Your Energy Levels**

   Assign a score to your energy level before and after each activity. Use a simple scale, such as 1 (completely drained) to 10 (fully energized).

3. **Analyze Patterns**

   At the end of the week, review your logs to identify patterns. Which activities consistently leave you drained? Which ones boost your energy?

4. **Take Action**
   - **Minimize Drains:** Look for ways to reduce or eliminate activities that deplete your energy. For example, set boundaries with draining individuals, streamline your workload, or declutter your environment.
   - **Maximize Boosters:** Schedule more time for activities that recharge you. Incorporate them into your daily routine, even in small doses.

The Path to Energy Mastery

By understanding where your energy goes and actively managing your energy drains and boosters, you set the stage for sustainable vitality. This energy audit is the first step in taking back control of your life, transforming it from one of exhaustion and overwhelm to one of focus, purpose, and flow.

The insights gained here will become the foundation for everything else you'll learn in this book. With a clear understanding of your current energy dynamics, you're ready to unlock the limitless reserves waiting within you.

Chapter 2: Daily Energy Hacks

Energy is like a current—it needs the right input and flow to stay strong and consistent throughout the day. In this chapter, we'll focus on simple, practical hacks you can implement daily to boost your energy in the morning and sustain it throughout the day. From powerful rituals to energy-sustaining foods and habits, you'll discover how small changes can yield transformative results.

Simple Rituals for Morning Energy Boosts

How you start your morning sets the tone for your entire day. The goal of a morning ritual is to jumpstart your physical, mental, and emotional energy, creating a solid foundation for everything that follows.

1. **Hydrate Immediately Upon Waking**

   After hours of sleep, your body is naturally dehydrated. Drinking a glass of water first thing in the morning replenishes your cells, jumpstarts your metabolism, and clears the mental fog. For an extra boost, add a squeeze of lemon to balance pH levels and support digestion.

2. **Move Your Body**

   Morning movement wakes up your muscles, boosts circulation, and releases endorphins that elevate your mood. Options include:
   - **Stretching:** Loosen tight muscles and improve blood flow with a 5-10 minute stretching routine.
   - **Yoga:** Practice a few energizing poses like Sun Salutations to awaken both your body and mind.
   - **Walking or Light Cardio:** A brisk walk or short workout can stimulate your energy for hours.

3. **Practice Intentional Breathing**

   Breathing exercises, such as deep diaphragmatic breathing or box breathing, increase oxygen flow to your brain and body. Spend

2-3 minutes focusing on your breath to center yourself and enhance your mental clarity.

4. **Gratitude Journaling**

Start your day with positivity by jotting down three things you're grateful for. This simple practice shifts your mindset, reduces stress, and generates emotional energy to tackle the day ahead.

5. **Expose Yourself to Natural Light**

Sunlight helps regulate your circadian rhythm, signaling to your brain that it's time to wake up. Step outside for a few minutes or open your blinds to let in the morning light. If sunlight isn't available, consider using a light therapy lamp.

6. **Set Daily Intentions**

Take a moment to visualize your goals and priorities for the day. This practice aligns your mental energy and gives you a sense of purpose, reducing wasted effort on unimportant tasks.

7. **Enjoy a Protein-Rich Breakfast**

Skipping breakfast or relying on sugary cereals leads to energy crashes. Opt for a breakfast rich in protein, healthy fats, and complex carbohydrates to stabilize blood sugar levels and sustain energy.

Foods and Habits That Sustain Vitality

While morning rituals set the stage, maintaining energy throughout the day requires mindful eating and consistent habits. Here's how to fuel your body and avoid the mid-afternoon slump.

Energy-Sustaining Foods

The food you eat directly impacts your energy levels. Choosing nutrient-dense options keeps you energized and focused for longer periods.

1. **Complex Carbohydrates**
   Unlike simple carbs that cause energy spikes and crashes, complex carbs provide a steady release of glucose. Examples include:
   - Oats
   - Sweet potatoes
   - Quinoa
   - Whole-grain bread

2. **Lean Proteins**
   Protein supports muscle repair and provides long-lasting energy. Incorporate:
   - Eggs
   - Chicken or turkey
   - Fish like salmon or tuna
   - Plant-based options like beans, lentils, and tofu

3. **Healthy Fats**
   Fats are an essential energy source, especially for sustained focus. Add these to your meals:
   - Avocado
   - Nuts and seeds (e.g., almonds, walnuts, chia seeds)
   - Olive oil
   - Fatty fish

4. **Fruits and Vegetables**

Packed with vitamins, antioxidants, and natural sugars, fruits and vegetables are excellent for energy:

- Bananas (great for a quick energy boost)
- Leafy greens like spinach and kale
- Berries (rich in antioxidants)
- Carrots and bell peppers for a crunchy, nutrient-dense snack

5. **Hydration**

Dehydration is a silent energy killer. Besides water, try energy-boosting beverages like herbal teas (e.g., green tea or peppermint) and coconut water for natural electrolytes.

6. **Energy-Enhancing Snacks**

Keep snacks handy to avoid energy crashes. Combine protein and healthy fats with natural sugars for an optimal mix:

- Apple slices with almond butter
- Greek yogurt with honey and granola
- Trail mix with nuts, seeds, and a small amount of dark chocolate

Energy-Sustaining Habits

In addition to eating the right foods, adopting the following habits ensures that your energy stays steady throughout the day:

1. **Take Regular Breaks**
   Working for long stretches without breaks leads to diminishing returns. Use techniques like the **Pomodoro Technique** (25 minutes of focused work followed by a 5-minute break) to keep your mind sharp and your energy high.

2. **Practice Micro-Movement**
   Sitting for extended periods slows circulation and saps energy. Every hour, stand up, stretch, or walk around for a few minutes to keep your blood flowing.

3. **Manage Stress Effectively**
   Stress is one of the biggest drains on energy. Incorporate daily stress-management practices such as:
   - Meditation or mindfulness exercises
   - Journaling your thoughts and feelings
   - Listening to calming music or nature sounds

4. **Limit Caffeine Intake**
   While caffeine can give you a temporary boost, overreliance leads to energy crashes later. Stick to one or two cups of coffee in the morning and switch to herbal teas or water for the rest of the day.

5. **Practice Energy-Positive Communication**
   Interactions with others significantly affect your emotional energy. Approach conversations with positivity, avoid gossip, and set boundaries with people who drain your energy.

6. **Create an Energizing Environment**
   Your surroundings play a huge role in how energized you feel.

Keep your workspace tidy, use uplifting colors or scents, and consider adding plants for a refreshing atmosphere.

7. **End Your Day Right**

Energy isn't just about what you do during the day—it's also about how you recover at night. A calming bedtime routine that includes activities like reading, meditating, or stretching can help you recharge effectively for the next day.

Putting It All Together

The key to daily energy optimization lies in consistent, intentional actions. Start your morning with energizing rituals, fuel your body with vitality-sustaining foods, and maintain habits that keep your energy balanced. These small but powerful hacks will transform the way you feel and perform every day.

Chapter 3: The Power of Recovery

In the pursuit of success, many people equate productivity with constant action. Yet, the most effective way to sustain high performance isn't to work harder—it's to recover smarter. Rest is not a sign of weakness; it's a vital tool for renewal and growth. In this chapter, we'll explore the transformative power of recovery, the importance of intentional rest, and techniques for quick mental and physical rejuvenation.

Rest as a Productivity Tool

Productivity isn't about how much you do but how effectively you use your energy. Without proper recovery, your performance suffers, creativity wanes, and decision-making falters. Rest is the secret ingredient that fuels sustained success.

1. **The Science of Recovery**

   Recovery isn't just about relaxation; it's about repairing and recharging your energy systems. Physically, recovery allows your body to repair muscle tissue, replenish energy stores, and regulate hormones. Mentally, it reduces stress, improves focus, and enhances memory consolidation. Without adequate recovery, your body and mind operate at a deficit, leading to burnout.

2. **The Myth of Constant Hustle**

   The "grind culture" glorifies non-stop work, but this mindset often leads to diminishing returns. Studies show that working long hours without breaks decreases efficiency and increases the likelihood of mistakes. Rest, on the other hand, allows you to return to tasks with renewed focus and energy, enabling you to achieve more in less time.

3. **Active vs. Passive Rest**

   Rest doesn't always mean doing nothing.

   - **Passive Rest:** Activities like sleeping, napping, or simply sitting quietly to allow your body and mind to recharge.

- **Active Rest:** Low-intensity activities such as walking, light stretching, or engaging in a creative hobby. Active rest can refresh your energy without fully disengaging from productivity.

4. **Benefits of Strategic Recovery**

Intentional recovery improves:

- **Productivity:** Restored energy allows for sustained high performance.
- **Creativity:** Downtime encourages the brain to form new connections, leading to innovative ideas.
- **Decision-Making:** A rested mind processes information more clearly and objectively.
- **Emotional Resilience:** Regular rest reduces stress and prevents emotional exhaustion.

Techniques for Quick Mental and Physical Recovery

Effective recovery doesn't always require long vacations or hours of downtime. You can incorporate quick, impactful recovery techniques into your daily routine to rejuvenate your energy.

Mental Recovery Techniques

1. **The Power of Micro-Breaks**

   Short, intentional pauses during your workday can significantly improve focus and energy. Examples include:
   - **The 20-20-20 Rule:** Every 20 minutes, look at something 20 feet away for 20 seconds to reduce eye strain and mental fatigue.
   - **Breathwork Breaks:** Spend 1-2 minutes practicing deep breathing exercises to calm your mind and increase oxygen flow.

2. **Mindfulness and Meditation**

   Mindfulness practices help you detach from stress and recenter your thoughts. Simple techniques include:
   - **5-Minute Meditation:** Sit quietly, focus on your breath, and let go of distracting thoughts.
   - **Body Scan:** Close your eyes and slowly bring your attention to each part of your body, releasing tension as you go.

3. **Visualization Exercises**

   Imagining a calm and peaceful scene, such as a beach or forest, can trigger your brain's relaxation response. Spend a few minutes visualizing this scene in detail, focusing on the sights, sounds, and sensations.

4. **Digital Detox**

   Screens are a significant source of mental fatigue. Step away from devices for a few minutes each hour to allow your brain to rest and recalibrate.

5. Creative Outlets

Engaging in creative activities like drawing, journaling, or playing a musical instrument provides a mental reset and taps into your brain's pleasure and reward centers.

Physical Recovery Techniques

1. Stretching and Mobility Work

Stretching releases muscle tension, improves circulation, and prevents stiffness from prolonged sitting. Incorporate dynamic stretches or yoga poses throughout your day, such as:

- Neck rolls and shoulder shrugs to relieve tension.
- Forward folds or hamstring stretches to loosen the lower back and legs.

2. Hydration Breaks

Dehydration can cause fatigue and impair physical recovery. Sip water regularly, especially after periods of intense focus or physical exertion.

3. Power Naps

A 10-20 minute nap can recharge your energy without leaving you groggy. Short naps improve alertness, memory, and mood, making them an excellent tool for midday recovery.

4. Massage and Self-Myofascial Release

Techniques like foam rolling or using a massage ball can reduce muscle tightness and promote relaxation. Focus on common tension areas like the back, neck, and shoulders.

5. Cold and Heat Therapy

- **Cold Therapy:** A cold shower or applying a cold compress can reduce inflammation and boost alertness.
- **Heat Therapy:** A warm bath or heating pad relaxes muscles and soothes physical tension.

Building a Recovery Routine

Recovery is most effective when it's consistent. Here's how to create a daily recovery routine:

1. **Morning Recovery Practices**
   - Start your day with gentle movement, hydration, and mindfulness to set a calm and energized tone.
2. **Midday Recovery Practices**
   - Incorporate a short walk, power nap, or stretching session to break up your workday and restore focus.
3. **Evening Recovery Practices**
   - Dedicate time to unwind with activities like reading, meditating, or taking a warm bath. Avoid screens and high-intensity tasks before bed to ensure quality sleep.
4. **Weekly Recovery Practices**
   - Set aside one day each week for deeper recovery, such as spending time in nature, engaging in hobbies, or practicing extended self-care routines.

The Synergy of Rest and Action

Recovery isn't a one-time event; it's an ongoing process that supports every aspect of your life. When you embrace rest as a productivity tool and integrate quick recovery techniques into your day, you create a sustainable cycle of energy and output.

Chapter 4: Focused Energy Application

Harnessing your energy effectively requires more than just having it—it's about using it wisely. This chapter delves into the art of focused energy application, teaching you how to identify your most productive hours and leverage them for high-impact tasks while avoiding the energy-sapping pitfalls of multitasking.

Using Your Best Hours for High-Impact Tasks

Every individual has specific times during the day when they feel most alert, energized, and focused. These are your **"peak performance hours"**—the times when your mental clarity and energy are at their highest. By identifying and utilizing these hours for your most critical tasks, you maximize your productivity and efficiency.

1. Understanding Your Energy Peaks and Troughs

Your energy fluctuates throughout the day based on your body's **circadian rhythm**—a natural cycle that governs sleep, wakefulness, and alertness. Recognizing these patterns helps you align tasks with your energy levels.

- **Morning Peaks:** Many people experience a sharp increase in focus and energy within an hour or two after waking.
- **Midday Dips:** A natural energy slump often occurs in the early afternoon. Use this time for lower-effort tasks or quick recovery techniques.
- **Evening Energy Spurts:** Some individuals, especially night owls, find their focus resurges in the evening.

2. How to Identify Your Peak Hours

- **Track Your Energy Levels:** For one week, log your energy, focus, and productivity every hour. Look for patterns in when you feel most alert versus when you struggle.
- **Experiment:** Try performing high-impact tasks at different times of the day to determine when you're most effective.
- **Consider Lifestyle Factors:** Your peak hours may depend on your sleep quality, diet, and stress levels, so adjust accordingly.

3. Prioritizing High-Impact Tasks

Once you've identified your best hours, reserve this time for your most important or challenging work. These are tasks that:

- **Require Deep Focus:** Complex problem-solving, strategic planning, or creative work.
- **Have Significant Impact:** Projects with long-term benefits or tasks critical to your goals.
- **Demand High Energy:** Activities that are mentally or emotionally taxing.

Action Plan:

- Create a "power hour" block each day where you focus solely on high-priority tasks.
- Eliminate distractions during this time by turning off notifications, setting boundaries, and creating a clutter-free workspace.

4. Batch Similar Tasks Together

Switching between unrelated tasks wastes mental energy and disrupts focus. Instead, group similar tasks into focused blocks, such as:

- Responding to emails or messages in one dedicated session.
- Scheduling all creative work (e.g., writing, designing) during your peak hours.
- Setting aside specific times for administrative tasks like invoicing or organizing files.

Avoiding Multitasking Energy Traps

Multitasking is often mistaken for efficiency, but research shows it's one of the biggest drains on productivity and energy. The human brain isn't designed to focus on multiple tasks simultaneously, and attempting to do so leads to mental fatigue, errors, and stress.

1. The Myth of Multitasking

When you multitask, you're not doing two things at once; you're rapidly switching your attention between tasks. This process, called "task-switching," consumes cognitive resources, leading to:

- **Decreased Efficiency:** Studies show that multitasking can reduce productivity by up to 40%.
- **Increased Mistakes:** Divided attention makes it harder to retain information and complete tasks accurately.
- **Mental Fatigue:** The constant switching wears out your brain, leaving you drained and unfocused.

2. Why Single-Tasking is Superior

Single-tasking—focusing on one task at a time—allows your brain to fully engage with the task at hand. Benefits include:

- **Improved Quality:** Greater focus leads to better results.
- **Faster Completion:** Concentrated effort often means finishing tasks in less time.
- **Enhanced Creativity:** Deep focus fosters innovative thinking and problem-solving.

3. How to Avoid Multitasking Traps

- **Limit Distractions:**
    - Turn off phone notifications or place your device in another room.
    - Use noise-canceling headphones or ambient sound to block out environmental distractions.
- **Set Clear Boundaries:**
    - Let colleagues or family know when you're unavailable.
    - Use tools like "Do Not Disturb" settings or status updates to indicate focused work time.
- **Work in Time Blocks:**
    - Break your day into blocks of uninterrupted focus. Use techniques like the **Pomodoro Technique** (25 minutes of work followed by a 5-minute break).
- **Prioritize Your Task List:**
    - Each day, identify your top three tasks and commit to completing them before moving on to less important ones.

4. Tools and Techniques to Support Focus

- **Task Management Apps:** Tools like Trello, Asana, or Todoist help you organize and prioritize tasks.
- **Focus Tools:** Apps like Focus@Will or Brain.fm provide concentration-enhancing background music.
- **Physical Reminders:** Use a timer, sticky notes, or a whiteboard to remind yourself to stay on task.

The Synergy of Energy and Focus

When you combine focused energy application with strategic task management, you create a powerful synergy. Instead of spreading yourself thin across multiple low-impact activities, you direct your energy toward meaningful work that drives results. The key is intentionality—being deliberate about when, how, and on what you spend your energy.

Actionable Steps for Focused Energy Application

1. **Perform an Energy Audit:**
   Review your daily activities and identify when you're most focused and productive.

2. **Establish Power Hours:**
   Schedule time during your peak hours for high-impact tasks, eliminating distractions and prioritizing deep focus.

3. **Practice Single-Tasking:**
   Commit to completing one task at a time and avoid the temptation to multitask.

4. **Use Tools to Support Focus:**
   Leverage apps, timers, and physical reminders to create an environment conducive to deep work.

5. **Review and Adjust:**
   Regularly assess your focus strategies and refine them as needed based on your energy patterns and workload.

Chapter 5: Sustaining High Energy Long-Term

Energy isn't just a resource you use to get through the day—it's the foundation of a fulfilling, vibrant life. To sustain high energy long-term, you must intentionally build a life that fuels you while protecting yourself from burnout. This chapter explores strategies for designing an energy-positive lifestyle and creating habits that keep your mental, physical, and emotional reserves replenished.

Building a Life That Energizes You

Sustaining high energy starts with aligning your life with activities, environments, and relationships that inspire and uplift you. This requires a holistic approach that prioritizes both external choices and internal mindset shifts.

1. Clarify Your Core Values and Priorities

Energy flows where your focus goes. If your daily life aligns with your core values, you'll naturally feel more energized. Misalignment, however, leads to frustration and fatigue.

- **Identify Your Core Values:** Reflect on what truly matters to you—family, creativity, health, adventure, contribution, etc.
- **Audit Your Commitments:** Are your current responsibilities aligned with these values? If not, consider delegating, reprioritizing, or eliminating tasks that drain you.
- **Set Energizing Goals:** Focus on goals that excite and inspire you. Break them into actionable steps to maintain momentum.

2. Create an Energy-Positive Environment

Your surroundings significantly influence your energy levels. A cluttered, chaotic environment drains energy, while a clean, organized space boosts focus and calm.

- **Declutter Regularly:** Remove unnecessary items from your living and working spaces. A tidy environment minimizes distractions and creates mental clarity.
- **Design for Comfort and Productivity:** Incorporate ergonomic furniture, good lighting, and elements that make you feel comfortable and inspired.
- **Infuse Nature:** Adding plants, natural light, or outdoor views can reduce stress and increase energy.

3. Cultivate Energizing Relationships

The people you surround yourself with either amplify or deplete your energy. Building meaningful, supportive relationships is key to sustaining long-term vitality.

- **Seek Positive Connections:** Spend time with people who uplift, motivate, and inspire you.
- **Set Boundaries:** Protect your energy by limiting interactions with negative or draining individuals.
- **Invest in Community:** Join groups or communities that align with your interests and values. Shared purpose fosters connection and enthusiasm.

4. Embrace Passion and Play

Engaging in activities that spark joy and curiosity fuels your emotional energy. Make time for hobbies, creativity, and exploration.

- **Discover New Passions:** Experiment with activities like painting, hiking, cooking, or learning a new skill.
- **Schedule Playtime:** Prioritize leisure activities as you would any other responsibility. Play is essential for emotional rejuvenation.
- **Celebrate Small Wins:** Recognize and reward your progress to maintain a sense of accomplishment and motivation.

Avoiding Burnout Through Lifestyle Design

Burnout is the result of prolonged energy depletion without sufficient recovery. To avoid it, you must design a lifestyle that balances effort with renewal, addressing the root causes of stress and fatigue.

1. Master Energy Cycles

Recognize and respect the natural cycles of energy expenditure and recovery. Avoid pushing yourself to the point of exhaustion.

- **Work Smarter, Not Harder:** Focus on high-impact tasks during your peak energy hours, and take regular breaks to recharge.
- **Schedule Recovery:** Incorporate daily, weekly, and seasonal recovery practices, such as short breaks, relaxing weekends, and vacations.
- **Listen to Your Body:** Pay attention to signs of fatigue and adjust your pace as needed.

2. Prioritize Self-Care

Self-care isn't selfish—it's essential for long-term energy sustainability. Make self-care practices a non-negotiable part of your routine.

- **Sleep Well:** Aim for 7-9 hours of quality sleep per night. Create a relaxing bedtime routine and maintain a consistent sleep schedule.
- **Fuel Your Body:** Eat a balanced diet rich in whole foods, lean proteins, healthy fats, and complex carbohydrates. Avoid energy-draining processed foods and excessive sugar.
- **Stay Active:** Regular exercise boosts physical and mental energy. Find activities you enjoy to make movement a sustainable habit.

3. Manage Stress Effectively

Chronic stress is a major energy drain and a leading cause of burnout. Learn to manage stress before it takes a toll.

- **Practice Mindfulness:** Techniques like meditation, deep breathing, and yoga calm the mind and reduce stress.
- **Simplify Your Life:** Eliminate unnecessary obligations, streamline routines, and focus on what truly matters.
- **Reframe Challenges:** Shift your mindset to see obstacles as opportunities for growth and learning.

4. Build Resilience

Resilience is the ability to bounce back from setbacks and adapt to challenges. A resilient mindset helps you sustain energy even during difficult times.

- **Cultivate Optimism:** Focus on solutions rather than problems and maintain a positive outlook.
- **Develop Emotional Intelligence:** Improve your ability to understand and manage emotions, both yours and others'.
- **Learn from Setbacks:** View failures as valuable learning experiences rather than permanent defeats.

5. Protect Your Energy from Overcommitment

Overcommitting is a common path to burnout. Learn to manage your time and energy wisely by setting boundaries.

- **Say No Strategically:** Don't take on tasks that don't align with your values or goals.
- **Delegate:** Share responsibilities with others to lighten your load.
- **Limit Perfectionism:** Striving for perfection can lead to unnecessary stress. Aim for excellence instead.

Long-Term Energy Strategies

To sustain high energy over the long term, adopt habits and practices that continually renew your physical, mental, and emotional reserves.

- **Stay Curious:** Keep learning and growing to maintain mental engagement and excitement.
- **Reflect and Adjust:** Regularly review your energy levels and lifestyle choices to ensure they're still serving you.
- **Celebrate Progress:** Recognize and celebrate milestones, both big and small, to maintain motivation.
- **Focus on Gratitude:** A gratitude practice shifts your perspective to abundance, reducing stress and increasing emotional energy.

Action Steps for Sustaining Energy

1. **Evaluate Your Current Lifestyle:** Identify habits, environments, or relationships that are draining your energy.
2. **Implement Energy-Positive Changes:** Start with one or two changes, such as decluttering your space or adding a weekly self-care ritual.
3. **Monitor Your Energy Levels:** Track how changes affect your energy and adjust as needed.
4. **Commit to Long-Term Growth:** Treat energy sustainability as an ongoing journey, not a one-time fix.

By building a life that energizes you and proactively protecting yourself from burnout, you'll create a sustainable foundation for long-term vitality. In the next chapter, we'll explore the synergy of mindset and energy, uncovering how your thoughts and beliefs can amplify or deplete your reserves. For now, reflect on what truly energizes you and start taking steps to design a lifestyle that fuels your best self.

Appendix A: Energy Planner and Recovery Tips

This appendix is designed to provide you with practical tools and actionable tips to plan, sustain, and recover your energy effectively. Use the energy planner to organize your day around your natural energy patterns, and explore the recovery tips to rejuvenate your mental, physical, and emotional reserves.

Energy Planner

The energy planner helps you align your daily tasks with your energy peaks and troughs, ensuring maximum productivity and minimal burnout. Below is a detailed template and instructions for using it effectively.

Daily Energy Planner Template

Time Block	Energy Level (High, Medium, Low)	Planned Activities	Recovery Actions
Morning (6 AM - 9 AM)			
Mid-Morning (9 AM - 12 PM)			
Early Afternoon (12 PM - 3 PM)			
Late Afternoon (3 PM - 6 PM)			

Time Block	Energy Level (High, Medium, Low)	Planned Activities	Recovery Actions
Evening (6 PM - 9 PM)			
Night (9 PM - 11 PM)			

How to Use the Energy Planner

1. **Identify Your Energy Levels:**
   - Spend a week observing your energy patterns. Note when you feel most focused (high energy), moderately productive (medium energy), or tired (low energy).
   - Use these insights to fill in the "Energy Level" column of the planner.
2. **Align Tasks with Energy Levels:**
   - Schedule high-impact tasks (e.g., problem-solving, creative work) during high-energy periods.
   - Reserve medium-energy periods for routine tasks like emails, meetings, or administrative work.
   - Use low-energy periods for rest, light reading, or planning for the next day.
3. **Incorporate Recovery Actions:**
   - For each time block, include at least one recovery action, such as a hydration break, a short walk, or a breathing exercise.
4. **Review and Adjust:**
   - At the end of each day, reflect on what worked well and what didn't. Adjust your planner to better fit your energy patterns.

Recovery Tips

Recovery is crucial for maintaining high energy levels. Below are categorized tips for mental, physical, and emotional recovery, along with quick practices you can integrate into your routine.

Mental Recovery Tips

1. **Practice Mindfulness:**
   - Spend 5-10 minutes focusing on your breath or observing your surroundings to calm your mind.
2. **Take Breaks:**
   - Use techniques like the Pomodoro Technique to schedule regular breaks. A 5-minute pause every 25 minutes can refresh focus.
3. **Declutter Your Mind:**
   - Write down lingering thoughts or tasks in a journal to free up mental space.
4. **Limit Digital Overload:**
   - Step away from screens for at least 10 minutes every hour. Use this time to stretch or take a brief walk.

Physical Recovery Tips

1. **Hydration:**
   - Drink a glass of water first thing in the morning and regularly throughout the day. Add electrolytes or herbal teas for variety.
2. **Stretching:**
   - Incorporate a quick stretching routine, focusing on tension-prone areas like the neck, shoulders, and lower back.
3. **Power Naps:**
   - Take a 10-20 minute nap during low-energy periods to recharge without feeling groggy.
4. **Massage or Foam Rolling:**
   - Use a foam roller or self-massage techniques to relieve muscle tension and improve circulation.

Emotional Recovery Tips

1. **Gratitude Practice:**
   - Write down three things you're grateful for each day to shift your emotional state and boost positivity.
2. **Positive Connections:**
   - Spend time with loved ones or call a friend who uplifts you. Emotional connection is a powerful energy booster.
3. **Laugh and Play:**
   - Watch a funny video, play with a pet, or engage in a fun activity to release stress and elevate your mood.
4. **Set Boundaries:**
   - Learn to say no to draining commitments and prioritize activities that replenish your emotional reserves.

Quick Recovery Practices

Sometimes, you need a rapid energy boost. Below are quick practices you can use to recover on the go:

1. **Breathwork:**
   - Practice box breathing: Inhale for 4 counts, hold for 4 counts, exhale for 4 counts, and hold for 4 counts. Repeat for 1-2 minutes.
2. **Mini-Meditation:**
   - Close your eyes and focus on your breath for 1 minute. Visualize a calm, peaceful place.
3. **Nature Break:**
   - Step outside for 5 minutes to soak in fresh air and natural light.
4. **Cold Water Splash:**
   - Splash cold water on your face or wrists to instantly refresh and invigorate.
5. **Quick Gratitude Check:**
   - Pause and mentally list three things you're grateful for in the moment.
6. **Movement Burst:**
   - Do 10 jumping jacks, a short dance, or a brisk walk around your space to get your blood flowing.

Reflection Prompts for Long-Term Energy Planning

Use these prompts regularly to ensure you're staying on track with your energy management:

- What activities consistently drain my energy, and how can I reduce or eliminate them?
- What habits or practices have the most positive impact on my energy levels?
- How well am I balancing effort and recovery?
- Are my daily actions aligned with my long-term goals and values?

By using the energy planner and incorporating these recovery tips into your life, you'll not only maintain high energy levels but also cultivate a lifestyle that supports sustainable productivity and well-being.

<u>Message from the Author:</u>

I hope you enjoyed this book, I love astrology and knew there was not a book such as this out on the shelf. I love metaphysical items as well. Please check out my other books:

-Life of Government Benefits

-My life of Hell

-My life with Hydrocephalus

-Red Sky

-World Domination:Woman's rule

-World Domination:Woman's Rule 2: The War

-Life and Banishment of Apophis: book 1

-The Kidney Friendly Diet

-The Ultimate Hemp Cookbook

-Creating a Dispensary(legally)

-Cleanliness throughout life: the importance of showering from childhood to adulthood.

-Strong Roots: The Risks of Overcoddling children

-Hemp Horoscopes: Cosmic Insights and Earthly Healing

- Celestial Hemp Navigating the Zodiac: Through the Green Cosmos

-Astrological Hemp: Aligning The Stars with Earth's Ancient Herb

-The Astrological Guide to Hemp: Stars, Signs, and Sacred Leaves

-Green Growth: Innovative Marketing Strategies for your Hemp Products and Dispensary

-Cosmic Cannabis

-Astrological Munchies

-Henry The Hemp

-Zodiacal Roots: The Astrological Soul Of Hemp

- **Green Constellations: Intersection of Hemp and Zodiac**

-Hemp in The Houses: An astrological Adventure Through The Cannabis Galaxy

-Galactic Ganja Guide

Heavenly Hemp

Zodiac Leaves

Doctor Who Astrology

Cannastrology

Stellar Satvias and Cosmic Indicas

<u>Celestial Cannabis: A Zodiac Journey</u>

AstroHerbology: The Sky and The Soil: Volume 1

AstroHerbology:Celestial Cannabis:Volume 2

Cosmic Cannabis Cultivation

The Starry Guide to Herbal Harmony: Volume 1

The Starry Guide to Herbal Harmony: Cannabis Universe: Volume 2

Yugioh Astrology: Astrological Guide to Deck, Duels and more

Nightmare Mansion: Echoes of The Abyss

Nightmare Mansion 2: Legacy of Shadows

Nightmare Mansion 3: Shadows of the Forgotten

Nightmare Mansion 4: Echoes of the Damned

The Life and Banishment of Apophis: Book 2

Nightmare Mansion: Halls of Despair

<u>Healing with Herb: Cannabis and Hydrocephalus</u>

<u>Planetary Pot: Aligning with Astrological Herbs: Volume 1</u>

Fast Track to Freedom: 30 Days to Financial Independence Using AI, Assets, and Agile Hustles

<u>Cosmic Hemp Pathways</u>

How to Become Financially Free in 30 Days: 10,000 Paths to Prosperity

Zodiacal Herbage: Astrological Insights: Volume 1

Nightmare Mansion: Whispers in the Walls

The Daleks Invade Atlantis

Henry the hemp and Hydrocephalus

10X The Kidney Friendly Diet
Cannabis Universe: Adult coloring book
Hemp Astrology: The Healing Power of the Stars
Zodiacal Herbage: Astrological Insights: Cannabis Universe: Volume 2
<u>Planetary Pot: Aligning with Astrological Herbs: Cannabis Universes: Volume 2</u>
Doctor Who Meets the Replicators and SG-1: The Ultimate Battle for Survival
Nightmare Mansion: Curse of the Blood Moon
<u>The Celestial Stoner: A Guide to the Zodiac</u>
Cosmic Pleasures: Sex Toy Astrology for Every Sign
Hydrocephalus Astrology: Navigating the Stars and Healing Waters
Lapis and the Mischievous Chocolate Bar

Celestial Positions: Sexual Astrology for Every Sign
Apophis's Shadow Work Journal: : A Journey of Self-Discovery and Healing
Kinky Cosmos: Sexual Kink Astrology for Every Sign
Digital Cosmos: The Astrological Digimon Compendium
Stellar Seeds: The Cosmic Guide to Growing with Astrology
Apophis's Daily Gratitude Journal

Cat Astrology: Feline Mysteries of the Cosmos
The Cosmic Kama Sutra: An Astrological Guide to Sexual Positions
Unleash Your Potential: A Guided Journal Powered by AI Insights
Whispers of the Enchanted Grove

Cosmic Pleasures: An Astrological Guide to Sexual Kinks
369, 12 Manifestation Journal

Whisper of the nocturne journal(blank journal for writing or drawing)

The Boogey Book

Locked In Reflection: A Chastity Journey Through Locktober

Generating Wealth Quickly:

How to Generate $100,000 in 24 Hours

Star Magic: Harness the Power of the Universe

The Flatulence Chronicles: A Fart Journal for Self-Discovery

The Doctor and The Death Moth

Seize the Day: A Personal Seizure Tracking Journal

The Ultimate Boogeyman Safari: A Journey into the Boogie World and Beyond

Whispers of Samhain: 1,000 Spells of Love, Luck, and Lunar Magic: Samhain Spell Book

Apophis's guides:

Witch's Spellbook Crafting Guide for Halloween

Frost & Flame: The Enchanted Yule Grimoire of 1000 Winter Spells

The Ultimate Boogey Goo Guide & Spooky Activities for Halloween Fun

Harmony of the Scales: A Libra's Spellcraft for Balance and Beauty

The Enchanted Advent: 36 Days of Christmas Wonders

Nightmare Mansion: The Labyrinth of Screams

Harvest of Enchantment: 1,000 Spells of Gratitude, Love, and Fortune for Thanksgiving

The Boogey Chronicles: A Journal of Nightly Encounters and Shadowy Secrets

The 12 Days of Financial Freedom: A Step-by-Step Christmas Countdown to Transform Your Finances

Sigil of the Eternal Spiral Blank Journal

A Christmas Feast: Timeless Recipes for Every Meal

Cosmic Sales: The Astrological Guide to Black Friday Shopping

Legends of the Corn Mother and Other Harvest Myths

Whispers of the Harvest: The Corn Mother's Journal

The Evergreen Spellbook

The Doctor Meets the Boogeyman

The White Witch of Rose Hall's SpellBook

The Gingerbread Golem's Shadow: A Study in Sweet Darkness

The Gingerbread Golem Codex: An Academic Exploration of Sweet Myths

The Gingerbread Golem Grimoire: Sweet Magicks and Spells for the Festive Witch

The Curse of the Gingerbread Golem

10-minute Christmas Crafts for kids

<u>Christmas Crisis Solutions: The Ultimate Last-Minute Survival Guide</u>

Gingerbread Golem Recipes: Holiday Treats with a Magical Twist

The Infinite Key: Unlocking Mystical Secrets of the Ages

Enchanted Yule: A Wiccan and Pagan Guide to a Magical and Memorable Season

Dinosaurs of Power: Unlocking Ancient Magick

Astro-Dinos: The Cosmic Guide to Prehistoric Wisdom

Gallifrey's Yule Logs: A Festive Doctor Who Cookbook

The Dino Grimoire: Secrets of Prehistoric Magick

The Gift They Never Knew They Needed

The Gingerbread Golem's Culinary Alchemy: Enchanting Recipes for a Sweetly Dark Feast

A Time Lord Christmas: Holiday Adventures with the Doctor

Krampusproofing Your Home: Defensive Strategies for Yule

Silent Frights: A Collection of Christmas Creepypastas to Chill Your Bones

Santa Raptor's Jolly Carnage: A Dino-Claus Christmas Tale

Prehistoric Palettes: A Dino Wicca Coloring Journey

The Christmas Wishkeeper Chronicles

The Starlight Sleigh: A Holiday Journey
Elf Secrets: The True Magic of the North Pole
Candy Cane Conjurations
Cooking with Kids: Recipes Under 20 Minutes
Doctor Who: The TARDIS Confiscation
The Anxiety First Aid Kit: Quick Tools to Calm Your Mind
Frosty Whispers: A Winter's Tale
The Infinite Key: Unlocking the Secrets to Prosperity, Resilience, and Purpose
The Grasping Void: Why You'll Regret This Purchase
Astrology for Busy Bees: Star Signs Simplified
The Instant Focus Formula: Cut Through the Noise
The Secret Language of Colors: Unlocking the Emotional Codes
Sacred Fossil Chronicles: Blank Journal
The Christmas Cottage Miracle
Feeding Frenzy: Graboid-Inspired Recipes
Manifest in Minutes: The Quick Law of Attraction Guide
The Symbiote Chronicles: Doctor Who's Venomous Journey
Think Tiny, Grow Big: The Minimalist Mindset
The Energy Key: Unlocking Limitless Motivation
New Year, New Magic: Manifesting Your Best Year Yet
Unstoppable You: Mastering Confidence in Minutes
Infinite Energy: The Secret to Never Feeling Drained
Lightning Focus: Mastering the Art of Productivity in a Distracted World
Saturnalia Manifestation Magick: A Guide to Unlocking Abundance During the Solstice
Graboids and Garland: The Ultimate Tremors-Themed Christmas Guide
12 Nights of Holiday Magic
The Power of Pause: 60-Second Mindfulness Practices
The Quick Reset: How to Reclaim Your Life After Burnout
The Shadow Eater: A Tale of Despair and Survival

If you want solar for your home go here: https://www.harborso-lar.live/apophisenterprises/

Get Some Tarot cards: https://www.makeplayingcards.com/sell/ apophis-occult-shop

Get some shirts: https://www.bonfire.com/store/apophis-shirt-emporium/

<u>Instagrams:</u>
@apophis_enterprises,
@apophisbookemporium,
@apophisscardshop
Twitter: @apophisenterpr1
 Tiktok:@apophisenterprise
Youtube: @sg1fan23477, @FiresideRetreatKingdom
Hive: @sg1fan23477
CheeLee: @SG1fan23477

Podcast: Apophis Chat Zone: https://open.spotify.com/show/5zXbrCLEV2xzCp8ybrfHsk?si=fb4d4fdbdce44dec

Newsletter: https://apophiss-newsletter-27c897.beehiiv.com/

If you want to support me or see posts of other projects that I have come over to: **buymeacoffee.com/mpetchinskg**
I post there daily several times a day

Get your Dinowicca or Christmas themed digital products, especially Santa Raptor songs and other musics. Here: **https://sg1fan23477.gumroad.com**

Apophis Yuletide Digital has not only digital Christmas items, but it will have all things with Dinowicca as well as other Digital products.

www.ingramcontent.com/pod-product-compliance
Lightning Source LLC
Chambersburg PA
CBHW060913130726
48001CB00006B/2223